Cover photograph:
brown shark.

Title page photograph:
hammerhead shark's jaw,
showing four distinct rows
of teeth.

THE SEA WORLD BOOK OF
SHARKS

BY EVE BUNTING
PHOTOGRAPHS BY FLIP NICKLIN

Harcourt Brace Jovanovich, Publishers
San Diego   New York   London

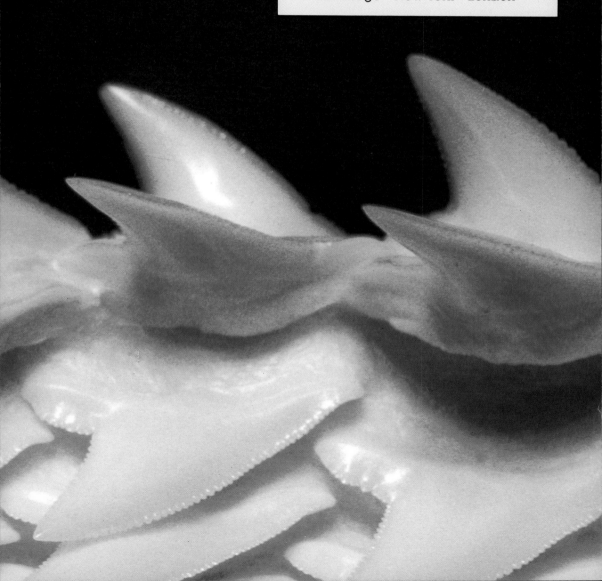

THE SEA WORLD BOOK OF SHARKS

Requests for permission to make copies of
any part of the work should be mailed to:
Permissions, Harcourt Brace Jovanovich,
Publishers, Orlando, Florida 32887

Printed in the United States of America

LIBRARY OF CONGRESS
CATALOGING IN PUBLICATION DATA

Bunting, Anne Eve.
   The Sea World book of sharks.

   Bibliography: p.
   Includes index.
   SUMMARY: Discusses the habits and
characteristics of sharks and introduces the
many kinds.
   1. Sharks – Juvenile literature.
[1. Sharks] I. Nicklin, Flip. II. Title.
QL 638.9.B83   597'.31   84-12950
ISBN 0-15-271947-4
ISBN 0-15-271952-0 (pbk.)

Additional photography credits

Doug Butner: pgs. 66-above (of a painting
by Mike Byergo and Ron Shunk)

David Doubilet: pgs. 16, 23-left, 40,
47-below, 48 and 71-below

James N. McKibben: pgs. 10, 27 and
43-below

Chuck Nicklin: pgs. 22, 29, 70-71-above
and 72-73

Sea World Photography Department:
pgs. 28, 32, 59, 60-61 and back cover

Ron and Valerie Taylor/Ardea London
Limited: pgs. 14-15, 20-below, 21, 56 and
66-below

A   B   C   D
    B   C   D   (pbk.)

CONTENTS

Dedicated to my friends
the librarians of
Pasadena, California,
for all the time
over all the years.

With special thanks to
Raymond S. Keyes,
Curator of Fishes
at Sea World in San Diego,
who generously gave
of his time and knowledge.

THE BEGINNINGS
CHAPTER ONE

Almost two hundred million years ago dinosaurs roamed the earth: the "terrible lizards" *Brontosaurus*, and *Stegosaurus*, and then the awesome *Tyrannosaurus*. *Pterodactyls* glided the skies on huge, leathery wings. In the sea were fish and crocodiles, a hundred feet long. And there were sharks.

Three hundred million years ago shallow seas covered earth where now there is land. The prehistoric fish *Dinichthys*, with its armor plating and powerful, crunching jaws, lived in those seas. There were fish. And there were sharks.

The dinosaurs are gone now. Our only records of them are bones in museums, or molds of giant footprints left in hardened mud.

The *Pterodactyls* are gone. We see the imprints of their bat-type bodies, like tracings on rocks. *Dinichthys* is gone. But there are still sharks.

   Dinosaurs may have disappeared because they could not adapt to the changing earth. Those creatures that survived on land and water did so because they could adapt. Sharks were among the fiercest fish and the swiftest swimmers in a world where only the strong could stay alive. Today they are "living fossils," relics of a time gone by.

   They swim now in all the oceans of the world, their great bodies shadowing the silent depths. There are millions of them — tropical sharks; polar sharks; sharks with small heads, like beavers; sharks that glow in the dark; dwarf sharks, just four inches long, that fit on the palm of the hand; and giant sharks that grow to a length of more than fifty feet. There are harmless sharks, sluggish sharks, and there are man-eaters — the most relentless hunters in the world . . . with the exception of humans themselves.

It is thought that sharks were among the first living creatures to develop teeth. Most others, including humans, followed their lead.

It is because of their teeth that we know as much about ancient sharks as we do. If we had looked to their skeletons for information, we would have found little. Shark skeletons then, as now, were not made of bone, but of cartilage. Cartilage is the tough, elastic material humans have between some bones. Cartilage does not last well. Prehistoric sharks decomposed on the floors of prehistoric oceans. They left little behind but the imprints of spines and fins, and fossilized teeth. Fortunately, many teeth have been found in fossil beds. From their shapes and sizes scientists can tell what kind of sharks they belonged to. By comparing the fossilized teeth with the teeth of living sharks, they can tell how the shark looked when it was alive.

One of the earliest sharks was *Cladoselache* (CLA-duh-sel-aich-ee) The remains of one were found a few miles from the city of Cleve-

Previous page: A brown shark, photographed from below.

Right: Two dwarf sharks, the smallest known sharks in the world.

Opposite page: Ancient and modern shark teeth. Both teeth are from great white sharks. The tooth on the left is fossilized, the tooth on the right is not.

land. They were buried in petrified mud. *Cladoselache* had a streamlined body, paired fins, open gill slits, and a mouthful of spiky teeth. It was four feet long and swam the seas in Devonian times (three hundred million years ago).

The monstrous *Carcharodon megalodon* (kar-KAR-oh-don MEG-oh-luh-don) lived in the oceans fifteen million years ago. Its name means "rough tooth/huge tooth." Huge indeed! Each tooth was as big as a human hand. Its reconstructed jaws are in the American Museum of Natural History in New York. They show a mouth large enough to swallow a small car. This would mean that the shark was gigantic. But the model jaws were done in scale with the teeth, and only some of the teeth were found. It's possible that the scientists who reconstructed the jaws may have made them a third too large. Even so, *Carcharodon megalodon* was a giant of the seas and a terror to any creature that shared its ocean.

The teeth of today's great white shark are almost identical to those of the prehistoric monster. So scientists know the great white is a close descendant. Recent dredgings of the Central Pacific have brought up more *Carcharodon megalodon* teeth. And these were not fossilized. They had not been there for that long a period of time. Could there still be a living *Carcharodon megalodon?*

One story tells us that a gigantic shark was seen by fishermen at Port Stephens, Australia, in 1918. They said it was "three hundred feet long at least" and a "ghostly, whitish color." A *Carcharodon megalodon*?

It is possible that sharks believed extinct are still swimming in our seas. In 1880 a Japanese fisherman found a strange looking shark. It was forty-two inches long and had a flat snout and pushed-out beak of a mouth. It was found to be a shark of a type thought to have vanished one hundred forty million years ago.

Who can say for sure that *Carcharodon megalodon* has gone forever? Could it be that in the deepest reaches of some deep dark ocean the monster still lives?

Shark! The very name is a mystery. When explorers first took their ships into strange waters, sharks were so rarely seen that there was no name for them. To early sailors the shark was only a moving shape behind the ship, a black fin cutting the blueness, a sudden flurry in the ocean when garbage was thrown over or when some poor seaman fell from the rigging.

For a long time the shark was called by its Spanish name, "*tiburón*." The English word "shark" did not come till later. It may have its roots in the German "*Schurke*," which means "villain," or in the Anglo-Saxon "*sceran*," which means "to cut." The French word for shark is "*requin*." Since the mass for the dead is a requiem, there would seem to be a connection. Was seeing a shark sliding through the ocean like seeing Death itself? In many parts of the world gray reef sharks are called requiems. Many scientists scoff at this explanation of the French name, but they don't seem to have a better explanation. It's just another mystery.

There are many things that we still don't know about these lords of the ocean. But we do know that they have been here since time began.

Human greed has destroyed many wonderful creatures of land and sea. The blue whale may soon be no more than a memory. But there are still untold numbers of sharks. They have changed since their early beginnings. They have adapted. And they have survived.

Reconstructed Carcharodon megalodon jaws, on display at Sea World in San Diego.

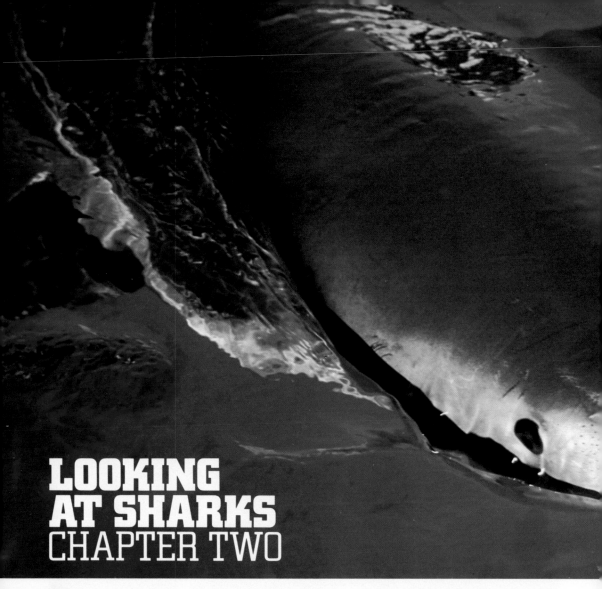

LOOKING
AT SHARKS
CHAPTER TWO

I t is difficult to describe "the shark." Different species of sharks
look different and act in different ways. So when we talk about
them, we must say "most sharks" or "some sharks" to allow for
their variety.

We can say that all sharks are fish with skeletons of cartilage, not
bone. Most have streamlined bodies that glide easily through the
water. They have been described as "torpedo shaped," or "missile
shaped." What they are is "shark shaped." The shark was here first,
and it had the original design.

Sharks do not have swim bladders to keep them afloat, as bony
fish do. It is because of its swim bladder that a goldfish is able to float

quietly in its bowl. Sharks are heavier than water. Most of them must swim, or sink. Sharks breathe by taking oxygen from the water that is forced into their mouths and out through their gill slits as they swim. They cannot go backwards. If they did, their oxygen would be cut off. Divers who work with sharks in adventure films often tow them backwards. This stresses the sharks so much that they are close to death and easy to handle. They can sometimes be revived by "walking" them forward again through the water.

The shark's liver helps it stay afloat. The liver sometimes makes up as much as 25 percent of the shark's weight, and it is very oily. Oil is lighter than water. The more a shark eats, the more oil its liver produces. So the lighter a shark is in the water. It works the other way around too. The longer a shark goes without food, the heavier it is in the water.

A simple, sweeping movement of the shark's tail is enough to keep it moving. Speed is not often necessary in the shark's life. Sharks are known as "sprinters" — slow movers who can speed up when they have to. "Stayers," such as whales and dolphins, swim fast for long periods of time.

Sharks have five, six, or seven gill slits on both sides of their heads. Their dorsal, or back, fins give stability. Their tails, or caudal fins, propel them forward. The upper fork of the tail is usually bigger than the lower one. This tends to tilt the head down as the shark swims. Its pectoral, or side, fins are basically rigid. They give "lift" — doing for the shark what the wings do on an airplane. If it were not

Previous page: A researcher watching and being watched by a great white shark.

Right: A young boy holding the liver of a large tiger shark.

Opposite page: A graceful blue shark showing its natural camouflage.

for this lift, the shark could ram right into the ocean's bottom.

Because these fins have to be rigid, it is difficult for sharks to put on the brakes. When they come up to something unexpected they usually dip or swerve to avoid it.

"The shark came out of nowhere."

"One minute the sea was empty. The next minute, I saw the shark."

These are the kinds of words we read in diving stories. Sharks are perfectly camouflaged as hunters of the sea. In the water they are generally drab colored. But in the right kind of light they can be a startling, beautiful amber. Their backs are usually dark, and their bellies lighter. Viewed from the surface, they blend with the darkness of the ocean. Viewed from below, their white bellies seem part of the light reflecting from above. The blue shark is blue, which isn't a bad sea color, and the white shark has a grey-brown back and a creamy white belly.

Some sharks have patterned skin, but never patterned in the dazzling colors of bony fish. The giant whale shark is red-brown with white or yellow spots and yellow lines on its back. But nature has not played a dirty trick on the whale shark. It too is camouflaged in its own special way. Light shimmering through water makes a pattern on what lies beneath. The pattern may look like lines or dots on the sand, or on the rocks or on the body of a great fish!

To see a shark sliding through the water is to see a sleek, smooth creature. But most sharks are not really smooth. They are covered

with "skin teeth," or denticles, which are small, sharp spines. The points slant toward the tail. The shark really is "all teeth, from stem to stern!" Scientists are not sure what these denticles are used for. They may be a way of protecting the shark's body. The skin teeth are, however, an extra danger to anyone in the water with a shark. Sharks like to bump an object before trying it out for taste. This may be caution, or curiosity. The denticles can scrape away skin, and blood is exciting to sharks. The skin of the shark can be stripped from the dead animal, treated, and used like sandpaper to polish wood. Then it is called shagreen (shuh-green).

There may be doubt as to the uses of the skin teeth. There is no doubt at all about the use of the teeth in the shark's mouth. They are not made for chewing. The shark does not chew. It swallows. It is simple for it to gulp down large chunks of meat. People have a thin pipe called the esophagus that food goes down on its way to the stomach. Try to swallow something too large and you choke. Sharks have scarcely any esophagus. The largest things can slip down quite easily. So sharks' teeth are made for cutting and holding. The cutting ones are triangular with jagged edges. The word "razor-sharp" has certainly been overused, but that's what the cutting teeth are. A crowd on a pier watched once as a man carefully shaved the hairs from his arm with the tooth of a tiger shark!

"Pavement teeth" are those used for seizing and crushing the food before it is swallowed. They are massive and almost flat — like

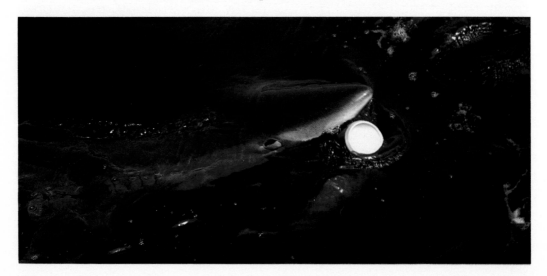

paving stones; thus the name.

Shark teeth, though so dangerous, are set weakly into the jaws. They can easily be lost from the gums, and sharks often leave a few behind when they bite into something hard. But whoever heard of a toothless shark? Five or six or seven rows of extra teeth lie in both jaws, one behind the other. When some are lost, the spare ones move forward into the gaps.

In olden days fossilized shark teeth were used to tell if food was poisoned. Rich men kept one on hand, just in case. To test for poison, the tooth was stuck into the food. If the tooth changed color there was poison indeed, and off with someone's head! Children in those times wore whale shark teeth around their necks at night. These were supposed to keep them safe, and to give them good appetites, so they'd grow big and strong too. And way back in time Hawaiian women studded their gloves with sharks' teeth. Sharktooth gloves were perfect for punching-out unwanted admirers.

Shark teeth are still sold. Souvenir shops in beach towns often have whole shark jaws for sale — large, gaping jaws studded with rows of pointed teeth. What kind of horrible hacking and sawing was needed to take them from the dead shark? Very little: shark jaws are not attached directly to the skull, but are held in place by ligaments and muscles. A bit of know-how, a sharp slice around, and the jaws are free.

Sharks do not all bite the same way when attacking something

Opposite page: A blue shark nudging a floating soft-drink can.

Left: A necklace made from an upper front tooth of an eighteen foot great white shark.

too large to be swallowed whole. Some slice away chunks of flesh while the front parts of their bodies shudder. Some snip with quick little pecks. Some twist and flop, and a great white will gulp piece by piece. Sometimes it won't swallow till its mouth is completely full — and that is quite a mouthful. Sharks do not need to roll over on their backs to bite, as was once thought. Although their mouths are set back on the underside of their snouts, they can attack head on. This is because the upper jaw is not fixed to the brain case. It can be raised and stuck out from the body. Sharks are rather messy diners, spreading blood and flesh around whenever they have to bite into something.

If they eat something that disagrees with them, such as a turtle shell, some sharks can bring their stomachs up and out through their mouths. After rinsing the lining in water, the shark can slip the whole

Right: A blue shark eating.

Below: A great shark ready to eat.

Opposite page: A great white shark, breaking the surface of the water, taking a piece of bait.

stomach back down again into place. It's rather like turning the lining of a pocket inside out, and is much better than suffering indigestion.

In the wild waters of oceans, lakes, and rivers big fish eat little fish to live. Big sharks eat big fish. They also eat littler sharks. This probably explains why sharks that are seen swimming together are usually about the same size. No little one is likely to try joining up with a group of larger ones. And because female sharks are generally larger than males, there are often groups of just one sex roving together. Many sharks seem to like to swim alone. Often they will come together to attack when there is a lot of easy food in the water. Then there can be the type of feeding frenzy that has been described so many times. But when the victim or victims have been eaten, the sharks will go their own secret, silent ways.

The shark does have companions, though. Small, blue-striped pilotfish often swim with sharks. And remoras — long, brown, green, or grey fish — will attach themselves to the shark's body. No one really knows why these two species risk being so close to sharks. Sharks scatter tidbits when they feed. So the pilotfish and remoras may be there for the crumbs the shark drops. Perhaps they also get protection from the giant fish. The pilots could be there for the easy

Right: A school of similar sized grey reef sharks.

Opposite page, left: A shark with a remora attached to its lower jaw.

Opposite page, right: researcher holding a one foot long remora, showing the suckers on the top of the remora's head.

ride on the bow wave the shark makes when it swims. Pilotfish do not guide the shark to its prey, as was once thought. Sharks don't need help in that department. The shark was supposed to be so grateful to the pilotfish that it didn't eat it. It's more probable that the pilotfish are too quick for the shark to catch, and too wary to get close to its jaws.

The company of the remoras is something else the shark can do nothing about. Remoras use the suckers on the tops of their heads to stick themselves to the shark. These suckers are so strong that in parts of the world fishermen use remoras to do their fishing for them. They attach a line to the remora's tail and throw it overboard in the direction of a turtle. The remora sticks itself on so firmly that the fisherman can just reel in his line, and he has dinner. Not much wonder the shark is stuck with remoras!

For millions of years sharks have been in the seas of the world. We know certain things about them: how they look, what they eat, and even how they taste. We have cut off their heads and sliced out their jaws. We have removed their insides and put their unborn babies in glass jars. We have read about, written about, and taken pictures of them. And still we know less of them than we know of almost any other living creature. That is their fascination — and their challenge.

STUDYING SHARKS
CHAPTER THREE

"You never know what a shark will do."
"Sharks are unpredictable."

People say these things, nod their heads, and look wise. They are partly right. We don't know exactly what a shark will do. But this isn't because they are crazy, mindless creatures. It is because we are ignorant of their ways.

It's hard to study live sharks. Many of them are shy of humans. Some of them swim a lot of the time at depths too deep for divers to reach — certainly too deep for divers to remain for stretches of time. Oceans and seas are not only deep but wide. And sharks are rovers. They range over great distances. Then too, there is danger to the

diver who may be following a shark to study it. The shark doesn't know that. It may feel threatened and attack, or it may speed up to get away. A shark can outswim any diver if it wants to.

Many land animals were once considered unpredictable. Jungles and forests are secret places too, but not as secret as the depths of the oceans. Zoologists have learned a lot in the last century about such creatures as wild apes. They were, of course, easier to study. One can sit all day in a tree with binoculars. Underwater is often dark and murky, trees are rare, and binoculars don't do much good! Neverthless, we are learning about sharks. And we will learn more. It is probable that when we do we will find them no more unpredictable than other wild creatures.

Dead sharks have been studied for years. It is the habits of the living creatures that still remain mysterious. We now know certain facts: the movement patterns of some species, the time and place of migration of others. But we still don't know enough.

Some sharks in the wild are "tagged" as are some birds and other animals. A shark to be tagged is caught and held alongside a boat. When it has been measured, a dart is stuck into its dorsal fin. The dart carries a tag. Each tag is numbered. The shark is released. If it is caught again, the finder is asked to return the tag to the research station. He is also asked to measure the shark, weigh it if possible, and tell how, when and where it was caught. This information helps us understand growth rate and living habits. One tagged blue shark was recovered four months later — 2,700 miles from where it had been tagged.

We need more than tagging alone to increase our shark knowledge. There is always the risk of poor return of tags. Or, with so many sharks in the ocean, the marked one may never be seen again. The ocean is immense. Taggers try to mark only big sharks. Smaller ones are often eaten. And a tag in a stomach doesn't tell much; except that its bearer ended up as a bigger shark's dinner! In one program where six thousand sharks were tagged only two hundred were recaptured.

Telemetering is also being used on sharks. Sometimes a transmitter is fixed to the shark's body with a dart. Or sometimes the shark

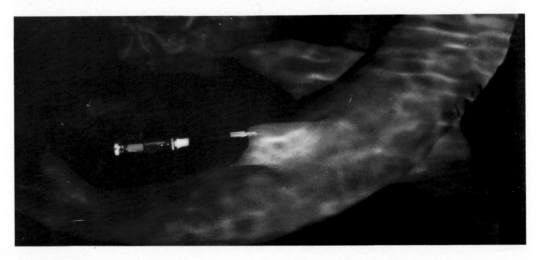

swallows the transmitter, hidden in food. The waiting boat follows the signals that come from the shark. Swimming speed can be checked, and the day and night shark habits compared. Telemetering has shown that blue sharks are more active at night.

Unfortunately, the ocean has its own natural noises. These can and often do mess up the man-made signals. In bad weather tracking is difficult. So is tracking a fast-moving shark. The signal can get weak with distance, then disappear; and the shark disappears along with it. A lost shark can take a long time to find, and tracking crews seem to tire before the shark does. There are other problems. A transmitter that has been swallowed can be irritating to the shark. It may simply throw it up to get rid of it.

A small underwater craft would be perfect for shark watching in the wild. It could go into depths beyond a lone diver's reach, have a long-lasting air supply, and move quickly and silently. And the person inside would be protected. Unfortunately, as yet there is no such perfect machine. There are underwater craft, such as the one-man wet-submarine designed by Dr. Donald Nelson of California State University, at Long Beach. But, it like others, is still in the early stages of development.

Since it is so difficult to go among sharks and stay there to study them, the answer seems simple. Bring the sharks to us. Then we can observe them more easily. Adding that knowledge to what we know of sharks in the wild would give us a good, rounded-out picture. Unfortunately, bringing sharks to us isn't easy either. Sharks that are

Previous page: A diver photographing a blue shark.

Opposite page: A lemon shark with a sonar telemetering tag attached to its dorsal fin.

Left: A researcher using a sonar tracking device.

strong and fierce in the water are fragile when handled. Their insides depend on water for support because their abdominal walls are thin. Even when a shark is gently pulled into a boat, examined, and returned quickly to the sea, it may die if it is handled incorrectly. Though it is easily injured, a shark is still dangerous when out of the water. It will thresh and snap. Its jaws and tail can do awful things to those around it. It will fight to survive. If it were different, sharks could not have lasted for many millions of years. Sharks that have had their insides removed have kept on living — for a while, anyway. One gutted body, thrown overboard, continued to swim and was caught again — on a hook baited with its own intestines.

A blue shark, horribly wounded, is reported to have hurled itself at a whale that was being held alongside a whaling boat. It died, literally, with its mouth full. The jaws of another shark lying on the deck of a research boat snapped shut when the head was touched. And at that time, the head had been separated from the body.

It's hard to believe that these savage creatures can be so frail out of the water, but they can. That makes them hard to move. But there are a few shark research centers worldwide where sharks are being taken from oceans and lakes and rivers and held for study.

Sea World in San Diego, California, has one of the newest shark

Right: A team of researchers carefully lifting a brown shark.

Opposite page: A group of researchers lifting a hammerhead shark into their boat.

research centers. There are eighty sharks there from sixteen different species.

Biologists and scientists are able to study such things as shark nutrition, and also the rivalries between the different species. Although this is not the same as watching them in the wild, a lot is being learned. Almost all of our recent knowledge on shark vision, hearing, and sense of smell has come from studies on captive sharks.

The large sharks at Sea World swim freely in the one hundred foot-long pool. Visitors can see them gliding underwater and get, perhaps for the first time, a picture of the shark as it really is — a beautiful, graceful, elegant creature. The usual round holding tank was not successful as a living area for captive sharks. The shark pool at Sea World is shaped like a flattened dumbbell with plenty of straight sides. This way the sharks can swim in straight lines instead of hugging the perimeter of a round area. They need to do this so their muscles can rest.

These sharks had been collected over a period of time before coming to San Diego. They were being held in large, lagoon-like pens at the Sea World's Shark Institute in Florida. A Sea World crew gathered the sharks and brought them to San Diego.

The lagoon was dragged with a large net to force the sharks into

the shallow area at one end. There the crew stood, knee-deep in the water with the struggling sharks. One by one they lifted and pushed the threshing creatures into waiting slings: dangerous work. There are ways other than lifting sharks by hand. But this is the safest way — for the sharks.

The animals were placed singly in special containers. Each container was an aquarium that looked like a big, blue box. Oxygen bubbled through the water in the boxes. The water flowed, moving through the shark's gills, just as though the shark were swimming. Each box had back-up power in case of a power failure.

The big Flying Tiger airplane waited at Miami. The boxes were

trucked to the plane and loaded by forklift. Inside, the plane soon looked as if it held a line-up of big, blue packing crates.

The six handlers worked constantly during the trip. Each shark had to be massaged to keep its blood circulating. This is something that the shark does for itself, naturally, as it swims. The boxes did exactly what they were designed to do: they kept the water and the sharks in, and they kept the sharks alive.

In San Diego the containers were transported to the waiting pool. Cranes lowered them into the water. When they were tipped up, the excited sharks swam free.

At Sea World the big sharks have no trouble living together.

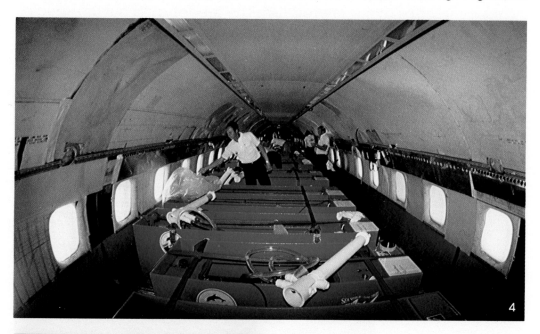

4

5

1. A bull shark being placed in a sling.
2. A sling being lowered into a special container.
3. The waiting plane.
4. Inside the plane.
5. A container being lowered into the shark pool at Sea World in San Diego.

They are fed three times a week from the open top of the pool. This part is behind locked doors and off-limits to the public. Each shark is hand fed, or rather, "tong" fed. The people who feed the sharks have buckets filled with vitamin-stuffed frozen fish. The sharks have all been tagged — the males on the right pectoral fin, the females on the left. As the feeders carry the buckets to the pool's edge, the sharks begin to come up. Soon the surface is moving with the black, wedge-shaped fins. The sharks know what's happening. They're ready.

The feeders kneel at the water's edge with their long, stainless steel tongs. The tagged sharks are easy to tell apart. As each one swims by it snaps at the offered fish. The feeder calls out the species,

A nine foot, two hundred and fifty pound lemon shark being tong fed at Sea World in San Diego.

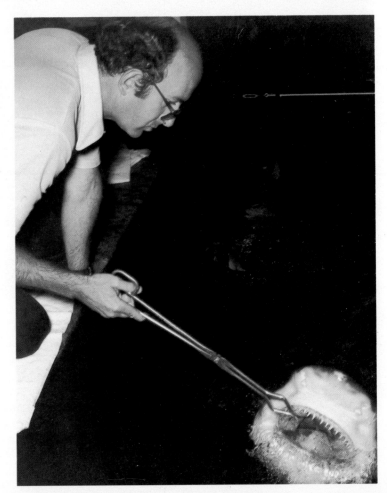

sex, and number. They have not given the sharks pet names. There's not a "Susie" or a "Harold" in the bunch. There is a "one, female, lemon," or a "two, male, bull," or a "six, female, brown." As the voices call out the types of sharks, a person with a clipboard keeps record. It is a tricky business, making sure each shark gets what it should and no more. Some are very aggressive and snap at each offered fish. If the fish is not for them, it has to be snatched away. The feeders say it is important that each shark gets enough, but not too much. They don't want fat sharks. And they certainly don't want hungry ones. Hunger would make for real danger in a life where shark eats shark.

The people who look after the sharks are cautious, but they don't seem afraid. They know these sharks, and they don't think they are unpredictable. They do accept, though, that they are working with wild creatures. They don't turn their backs on the pool. And they keep their hands out of the water. If an accident did happen and one of them fell in, there is a chance he or she could escape unharmed. They know the sharks and they know what to do — stay cool, don't splash, don't show fear, move slowly and quietly to the edge of the pool. If someone else fell in, it would be different. Death could come in a very few minutes.

The Sea World sharks seem content, and it is good that they do because these sharks could never be turned free in the ocean. They are now unafraid of humans and might come in to beaches where people swim. The people would be terrified, and rightly so. These sharks are almost all from species known to have attacked humans. Sharks are carnivores — meat eaters. They are also predators, who hunt for their food. So are lions and tigers and leopards. The great cats know no more of mercy than the shark does. They have probably attacked as many people as sharks have. The cats are feared, but they are not hated. They are admired.

The lion is the king of the beasts.

There is poetry written about the tiger, who is the "Tyger! Tyger! burning bright./ In the forests of the night."*

What of the sharks? Aren't they as terrible, as wonderful?

It will be good if our new and growing knowledge leads to a new understanding, and our understanding to new respect.

*From the poem *The Tyger* by William Blake.

THE SENSITIVE SHARK
CHAPTER FOUR

The shark is sometimes called "the swimming nose" because of its wonderful sense of smell. It should be called "the swimming computer." All of its senses work together to make the shark supersensitive to all that is happening in the ocean around it.

The shark's ability to smell is uncanny. Two-thirds of its brain is devoted to that sense alone. The smelling is done through the nostrils, which are usually on the underside of the head, and which have nothing whatever to do with the shark's breathing.

An experiment was done to test the shark's sense of smell. Two separate tanks were used: one held sharks, and the other held fish. While the fish were swimming quietly, water was piped from their

tank to the sharks' tank. The sharks showed little interest. Then the fish were prodded to make them frightened. When some of this water was piped in to the sharks, things livened up. The sharks began circling and snapping at the pipe that carried the fear-scented water! This is scary news for fish.

Scarier for humans were the results of another test. These showed that sharks can smell one drop of human blood in one hundred million drops of water. Any type of blood excites sharks. Skin divers who spear fish and tie them to their belts are asking for trouble. Many attacks on skin divers come at waist level. The shark has been alerted by the blood of the struggling fish. It follows its nose. And the human is there too when the shark lunges and bites.

Scientists were encouraged when they found that sharks didn't like the smell of human sweat. They tried making an artificial "sweat smell" as a shark repellent. Unfortunately, it didn't work all the time. What turns one shark off may turn another on. There are just too many kinds of shark nosing around.

We once thought that sharks were good "smellers" but bad "see-ers." We were wrong. Now we know that most sharks see quite well. But sharks hunt mainly in the dark of night. So they use their other senses first to find their prey. Then they use their eyes as they near it.

Sharks' eyes differ in size, shape, and color. They have probably evolved that way to meet different needs. The eyes of some appear to glow in the dark, like the eyes of cats. Some have eyes as green as emeralds, and the eyes of the great white have been described as flat and black and empty.

Behind the eyes lie layers of cells — silvery plates, like mirrors. These intensify what the shark sees in dim light. Upper and lower immovable eyelids partially protect the eyeball. Some species have another, lower eyelid which can move. It is called the nictitating membrane (Nik-tit-tate-ing mem-brain). Sharks can use it to totally cover their eyes for more protection. They have been seen with their nictitating membranes closed while eating stingrays. Who wants a poisonous spine in the eyeball?

Sharks do not see colors as we see them. In fact, it is probable that they are colorblind. They can, however, distinguish between a light color and a dark one. Greek divers working off the Florida coast wear dark clothes. They tuck their hands under their armpits if sharks come close. Sharks, they say, like light colors. Japanese pearl diving women wear jackets, skirts, and hoods of shining white. They say everyone knows light colors keep sharks away. No one knows.

A military plane that crashed in the Pacific sank so quickly that the crew had to take to the water. Some of the men wore orange flying suits. Others wore green. Only those in the green suits were rescued. The others had all died, victims of shark attacks.

Researchers who work with sharks and color call bright yellow and orange-yellow "yum-yum yellow" for grisly reasons. These are the colors used for life rafts and jackets. They contrast with the sea and can be easily spotted by searchers. It seems they can also be easily spotted by sharks. And it seems too that this brightness is attractive to them. It is difficult to be certain. There are too many kinds of sharks to be certain about their likes and dislikes.

Many of them do seem to be curious about things that shine. Bracelets and rings are often found on arms or hands that have been bitten off and recovered from sharks' bellies.

"The Silent World" that lies deep in our oceans is not silent at all. It seems that way to us because most underwater sounds are too high or too low for our ears to pick up. Sharks have no such problem. Their ears are usually behind their eyes and are open to the sea. But the shark does not depend on its ears alone to hear. Small canals run the length of the shark's body. These are under the skin, and they are filled with fluid. Using these, the shark can gather in the sounds and movements in the water around it.

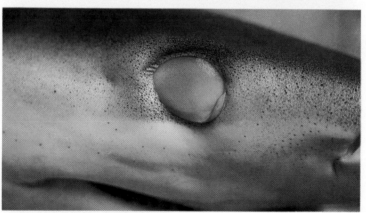

Previous page: A blue shark.

Left: Two close-up photographs of a blue shark's nictitating membrane. The photograph above shows the membrane as it begins (starting from the bottom of the eye) to close over the eye, and the photograph below shows the eye completely covered.

Struggling fish make low-frequency sounds that sharks can hear from hundreds of yards away. Even a recording of fish sounds brought sharks to snap and throw themselves at the loudspeaker. Blasting underwater can bring sharks. So can the sounds people make after a shipwreck or when a plane ditches at sea. Sharks are also attracted by the sounds a helicopter makes. A hovering chopper trying to help in a sea rescue would be better hovering somewhere else.

Superb hearing, good vision, an incredible sense of smell: what more does the shark need for survival? Probably nothing. But it is equipped with some extras. On its snout are small, black pores. With these the shark can sense small electrical changes in the water. All living things give off electrical charges. So these "ampullae of Lorenzini" (amp-u-lie of Law-ren-z-nee) must make it even easier for the

shark to find its prey. Another "extra" the shark has is its sensory pits, which run along the side of the shark's body. These sense vibrations in the water.

We know a little about the shark's sense of taste. Taste buds have been described in the mouths and throats of some species. These species seem to prefer certain foods to others. They will spit something back, probably because they don't like the way it tastes, for example, a squid that was soaked in alcohol in an experiment. Perhaps that is why they've been known to release a person covered with suntan oil or wearing a rubber suit.

Most sharks don't like rotting food, particularly rotting shark. Although, when decayed shark flesh was tried as a repellent, it didn't work. Sharks, probably like people, have different tastes. They do seem to like live shark meat — maybe because even a small shark is big enough to satisfy a large appetite, or maybe because sharks like that shark flavor!

There are few things too tough or nasty for the shark to try. Stingray spines, poisonous to other sea creatures, are found all the time stuck in sharks' jaws or bellies. One shark had a tooth bud that had been split in two by a stingray spine. All the reserve teeth in the rows behind it were deformed too. But the shark stayed healthy — until someone killed it.

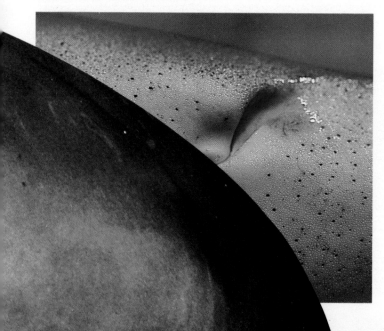

Far left: The head of a lemon shark showing the ampullae of Lorenzini around the nose.

Left: A close-up photograph of the nostril and the ampullae of Lorenzini.

There seems to be only one thing a shark can't eat: a small, flat fish called the Moses sole, which is found in the Red Sea. In its fins are glands which contain a white, milky fluid. This fluid seems to paralyze the shark's jaws. When it tries to gulp down a Moses sole, its mouth won't close. The shark swims frantically, jaws agape, and the little flat fish floats out and away. Scientists are studying the Moses sole. It could be, at last, a breakthrough in that hard-to-find shark repellent.

There is no accounting for taste, and the strange things that have been found in shark bellies. In the sixteenth century soldiers still wore armor. It was reported that at Marseilles, France, great whites were caught which had in their stomachs, "whole men in *armor*"! A roll of tar paper was taken from a dead shark's stomach, a keg of nails, a yellow-billed cuckoo. There was a bottle of wine that a trawler crew found and drank with gusto. They said it was very old and very fine indeed.

The unexciting truth is that sharks mostly eat normal shark food: fish, squid, crabs, and mollusks. Of the thousands and thousands of dead sharks whose stomachs have been searched, few held anything unusual. It's the ones that did that made the headlines. One story tells of a fisherman who found a straw hat, dried it out, and wore it thereafter for all the fishing days of his life.

Human remains are sometimes found — grisly, gruesome, sickening! In fairness to the shark, we have to say that we don't always know if the person was eaten alive, or already dead when found by

the shark. One shark spat up a human arm. It had a tattoo on it which made it easy to identify. The police had been looking for the man whose arms had been tattooed in just that way. He had been murdered and dumped in the ocean. And it wasn't the shark who murdered him.

Unfortunately, we do sometimes know just how the human remains got into the shark's belly. In 1916 there were several shark attacks off the coast of New Jersey. A shark was caught twelve days later. Its stomach gave up a mass of still identifiable human parts.

Sharks, like most carnivores, will eat whatever meat is available, when it's available. But human flesh is not a shark's natural food. If it were, there would be a lot of unhappy sharks. They don't come across people in the oceans every day. Experts think sharks don't like the way humans taste. If they did, they would come in more often to beaches where people swim. Sharks are good at finding and remembering easy food sources — places where garbage is dumped, a fish processing plant that gets rid of its wastes in the water. Sharks find these places quickly and hang around them. They don't hang around swimming beaches. When one does it makes history.

Some scientists say that when shark bites a human it is a mistake. The shark is not expecting the person to be there. It thinks it has found a seal or a large, slow fish. Often the arm or leg is spat out after it is bitten off. So the experts may be right. Attacks on humans may be only a mistake. Or the mistake could be ours for being there — in that underwater world where the sensitive shark is king.

A reef whitetip shark avoiding a Moses sole.

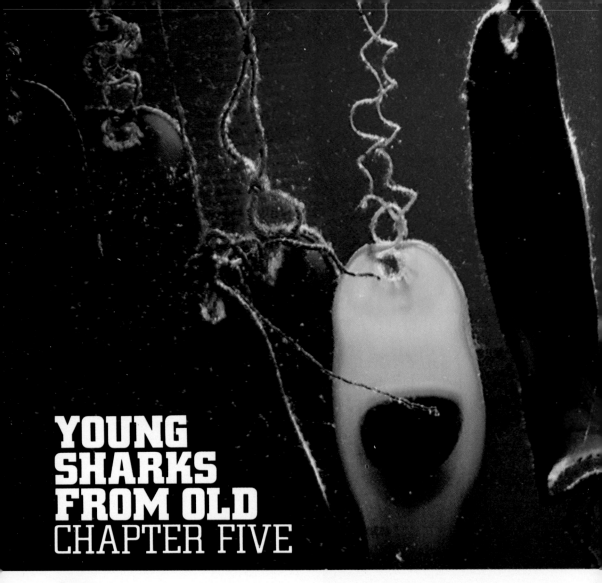

YOUNG
SHARKS
FROM OLD
CHAPTER FIVE

Sharks do not easily give up their secrets. They have seldom been seen mating. Once lemon sharks were observed while mating, and there is one photograph of mating horn sharks. But the big rovers of the open seas are well able to guard their privacy.

We do know that during mating season some species of sharks come together in groups of hundreds of individuals. These normally solitary animals mate and then go their separate ways once again. (There are no happy families in the shark world.) The mating process itself seems to be rough. "Mating scars" are often found on female sharks. These are caused by the male as he grasps the

Above: Ten swell shark egg cases at different stages of development. The strands at the top of the egg attach the case to plants on the sea bottom.

Left: A grey reef shark with mating scars on its back.

female either by the back or by the pectoral fin to hold her into position.

Male sharks have twin organs called claspers, which release sperm into the female. These claspers point to the rear. During mating they turn forward so they can enter the female's vent. The male uses only one clasper while mating. The claspers of each species are a little different. They match up with the vents of the females of that species and no other. So tiger sharks can't mate with threshers, for example; or makos with great whites. The eggs are fertilized inside the female's body.

Sharks can be divided into three groups. Those that are *oviparous* (oh-VIP-uh-ruhs). That means the fertilized eggs are pushed out by the mother. She leaves them, and they hatch in the water. Horn sharks, cat sharks, some carpet sharks, and whale sharks are oviparous.

The second group is those sharks that are *ovoviviparous* (oh-voh-vigh-VIP-uh-ruhs). That means they bear live young from eggs hatched inside their bodies. Tiger sharks, porbeagles, makos, sand tigers, and spiny dogfish are all ovoviviparous.

The third group is *viviparous* (vigh-VIP-uh-ruhs). The young grow and live inside the mother without a shell, and are born live. Hammerheads, smooth dogfish, basking sharks, and blues are examples of viviparous sharks.

The first group, oviparous sharks, drop their eggs in the water after fertilization. Each one is protected by a tough egg case. Some cases have tendrils that twine themselves in seaweed. Others have horns and sticky undersides so they can attach themselves to rocks or sand. The "mermaid's purse," which is sometimes washed up on beaches, is the egg of a swell shark. Sea water flows in and out of the egg case bringing oxygen to the embryo (EM-bree-oh) — the unborn baby.

Shark eggs are rich in yolk, and the embryos feed on these yolks. They grow in much the same way that birds grow in bird's eggs. When the eggs hatch, about six to eight months after they're dropped, the babies swim away. Immediately they start on their

A swell shark egg case showing the embryo and the yolk. As the embryo grows, it feeds off the yolk until the embryo fills the case and the yolk is gone. At birth a four inch long baby shark leaves the egg case from the bottom.

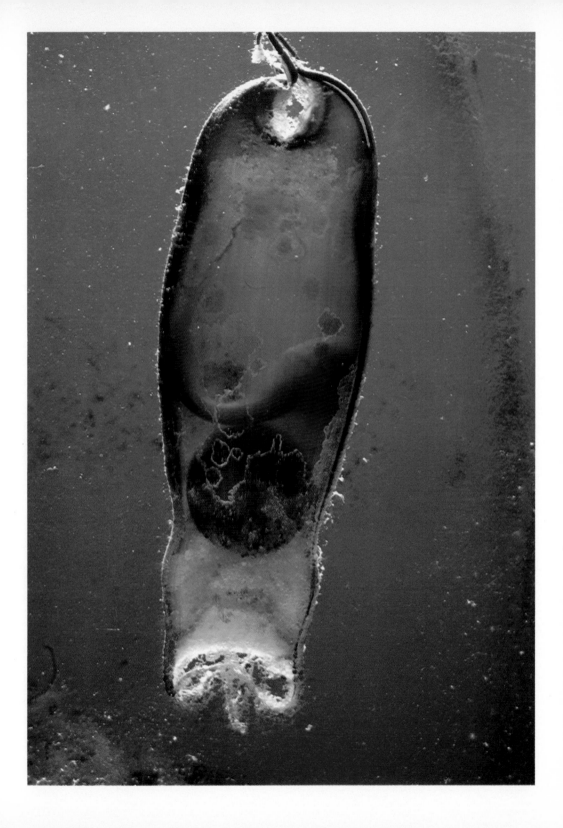

lifelong search for food.

The largest shark egg ever found was hauled up from the depths of the Gulf of Mexico. It was twelve inches long. When it was slit open, a fourteen-and-a-half-inch-long whale shark embryo was found inside. It was perfect in every way — exactly like mother — even to the lines and spots on its back. This was the first time a whale shark egg had been found, and none have been found since. But at least we now know that the whale shark is oviparous.

The eggs of the second group, ovoviviparous sharks, have thin, fragile shells. They hatch inside the mothers. The embryos feed on the yolks until these are used up. Then they are fed by a creamy fluid that comes from the mother's internal glands. When they are fully formed, the babies are born. In some ovoviviparous sharks, the babies that hatch early feed on the yolks of the unhatched eggs. Sand tiger and porbeagle sharks are often born all bloated and pudgy from eating all that egg yolk. They are said to have "yolk stomachs." Sometimes the early hatched babies eat each other. In

South Africa one unborn baby six and a half inches long was found with its one-and-a-half-inch brother in its belly!

While he was examining a sand tiger shark one day, a researcher put his hand into the female's vent and was bitten. The unborn baby's teeth were still soft and weak and didn't cut his skin, but he felt the nip. That instinct to bite seems to be developed before birth.

In viviparous sharks, the third group, the embryos have no egg shell. So they don't have to hatch, inside or out. The embryo is attached by a cord to a yolk sac, which is attached to the mother. At birth the yolk sac breaks and the young shark is born. We are not sure how long the embryos develop inside before they are ready to be born. It is probably quite a long time. We do know that in the spiny dogfish twenty-two to twenty-four months pass between fertilization and birth.

Newborn sharks are called pups, which is a playful-sounding name for such fierce little creatures. Litters vary in size. A thresher

Opposite page: Two young swell sharks.

Left above: An embryonic male hammerhead shark.

Left below: Three unfertilized tiger shark eggs (eggs that do not carry embryos.)

may have only two to four pups. A tiger shark can have as many as eighty-two. The babies are large. Great white pups are usually just over four feet long. There have been reports of attacks on humans made by great whites so small that they must have been less than a year old.

When female sharks are ready to give birth, they frequently go off alone into shallower water. Some species do not eat for a few days after the birth — a good thing for the survival of the species! And males don't go near the nurseries, which is another good thing for the babies. The male sharks have not at this time lost their appetites, and all those little mouthfuls would be a temptation.

Nature takes care of the babies before, during, and after birth. It also takes care of the mothers. Some baby sharks are known to turn around inside and face toward the mother's tail before they are born. Then they come out head first into the sea. That way their denticles point in the right direction. They go "with the grain" instead of against it, which must be a relief for the mother. The sharp spines of baby dogfish have knobs on them at birth. That way the mother doesn't get jabbed as the babies slide out. Afterwards the knobs simply drop off.

The mother shark does not hang around for long after the birth, which is just as well. Her appetite returns quickly. Mother shark love seems to be missing entirely, although some fishermen say the thresher is an exception. They say she stays with her young and swims beside them. She shelters them under her pectoral fins at the first sign of trouble, like the mother hen drawing her feathers around her chicks. It's a pretty picture, but it's not likely that it's true.

Young sharks are well able to take care of themselves. (A few are born deformed. They have no mouths, or their eyes are not set right, or they have some body deformities. These weak ones will not last long.) Normal babies have full sets of biting teeth. Their senses are all in good working order. They don't need mother's protection. From the moment of birth they are tough and fast and savage. From the beginning they are more dangerous than in danger.

A litter of tiger shark pups.

SOME SHARKS
CHAPTER SIX

Sharks are found all over the world, in oceans cold and warm. One kind is even found in lakes and rivers. As of now, we know there are close to three hundred species. There may be more.

In cold waters there are fewer species of sharks, but there are more sharks to be found in each species. In warmer (temperate and tropical) waters there are more species of sharks, but fewer numbers in each species. Tropical waters abound with sharks. There are so many that if they all ate the same food at the same times the supply would dwindle. Instead, there are all types of sharks. There are those that grub only on the bottom. There are those that feed only on the top. Some prowl the reefs by day; some by night. There are fast

swimmers and slow swimmers. This way there is less competition for food and for space.

Greenland sharks, sometimes called sleeper sharks, live in cold, cold waters and often swim under ice. They are big creatures, commonly about sixteen feet in length. But they are so sluggish that they are easily caught.

Eskimos fish for them by making a hole in the ice and letting fish blood ooze into the water. The blood brings the shark, and it can be harpooned and dragged out. It is like a log when pulled from the water, and it is no more dangerous. The greenland shark may get its revenge on those who kill it. Its flesh is poisonous unless cooked for a long time in many changes of water. Those who eat it without knowing what to do are in for a shock. They look as if they're drunk. Even dogs who have a hunk or two will stagger and vomit. The Eskimo word for "drunk" is "shark sick." They probably saw the results of eating greenland sharks before they saw the results of alcohol!

Greenland sharks are brown-gray above and below. They are viviparous. One sixteen-foot female had ten embryos in her body.

The **basking shark** lives mainly in temperate (fairly cool) oceans, but it can also be found in colder waters. It is the second largest fish in the world and grows to a length of forty five feet. That's bigger than a bus! The basking shark is a plankton eater and doesn't need teeth to catch its prey. So its teeth are the smallest things about it. It has five long gill slits. Inside, on the gill arches, are more than a thousand gill rakers, through which it sieves plankton. It often swims with its mouth open, sucking in all the minute creatures that swirl around it. And it sucks in plenty. A ton of plankton has been found in a basking shark's stomach. Better think twice before you slice one open!

These sharks often travel in schools, like a herd of great, underwater elephants. Sometimes they cruise in circles, or single file on the surface, head to tail. Their snouts

Previous page: One lemon shark on the left, and four brown sharks on the right.

Above: A basking shark.

are often rubbed raw from bumping the denticles of the tails in front. It isn't hard to imagine where the stories of sea serpents started. Think of all those curved backs, all those pointed fins, all that churning ocean!

A great "sea snake," fifty-five feet long, was found in 1808 on the Orkney Islands, off the coast of Scotland. It was washed up on a beach, and it had a "horse's mane, a long neck, and six legs." The snake was probably a decomposed basking shark. The pectoral fins, pelvic fins, and claspers could be mistaken for legs. The mane could have been the frayed remainder of the gill slits. This explanation is not so romantic, but more likely. Basking sharks have been found dead on beaches. Since sharks don't have air bladders to keep them afloat, they are supposed to sink when they die. Perhaps basking sharks strand themselves as whales do. We don't really know.

Gigantic as they are, basking sharks can leap all the way up and out of the water. It's hard to picture those tons and tons of flesh shooting up and splashing back, the cold green watery walls rising on either side, the waves rolling and spreading from the slap of the mammoth body. Why do they make such an effort? It may be to get rid of parasites on their skin, or a way of signalling to other basking sharks, or simply because they like to jump. Only another basking shark knows for sure.

No one knows either where they go in the wintertime. In winter, basking sharks, like flies, simply disappear. They are seen in great shoals off the British Isles in summer. They are not seen again till spring of the next year. Plankton is scarcer in winter than in summer. The basking sharks may shed their gill rakers then. By the following spring new rakers have grown. Perhaps these great beasts rest on the sea bed, waiting while their "food sieves" grow, sleeping and dreaming their own shark dreams.

Basking sharks are viviparous. Their snouts are pointed, and they have triangular dorsal fins.

There are probably more **blue sharks** than any other kind in temperate oceans. The blues can grow to about twelve feet long, and are sleek and graceful. Their snow-white undersides are separated from the vivid blue of their backs by a broad, silvery band. Their snouts are long. So are their bodies, their tails, and their pectoral fins; and they can glide and swoop through the water. Their upper jaws are so filled with teeth that the base overlap. Blues sometimes put these teeth to bad use: they have been convicted of eight attacks on humans. The chances are that they are guilty of many more. When the troop ship *Nova Scotia* sank off South Africa, there were more than a thousand persons on board. Many were killed or injured by sharks in the water. The sharks may have been blues.

Blue sharks are the ones most often mentioned in tales of old whaling ships. That is why they are called "blue whalers" in Australia. In those days sailors thought that when someone on board was

dying, a blue shark would mysteriously appear to swim beside the ship — not too happy a sight, I'm sure, if you were feeling poorly! The shark was supposed to disappear as soon as the sailor died and the body was thrown over for a "burial at sea."

Blues are viviparous. The largest number of embryos found in a female was eighty-two. In death, blues pale and lose their bright color, fading quickly to a dull, drab gray.

Mako sharks swim in temperate waters too. They are also blue, but richer and deeper, and their bellies are also white. They are slender, fast, and graceful. The mako has been described as "blue muscle," and as looking as if it were "poured into its skin."

Their speed and grace come in part from their body temperature. Along with porbeagles, and possibly great whites, makos have blood temperatures warmer than the sea around them. Warm blood makes for warm muscles, blue or otherwise. And warm muscles make for speed.

A mako can jump fifteen to twenty feet in the air when it's excited. Makos will charge boats. Sometimes they will leap right into them. One shark fisherman tells of the time that happened to him. The mako landed in his boat. It bounced and twisted, slamming itself from side to side. It smashed fishing chairs and tore rod holders loose. And all the time the fishermen were twisting and jumping themselves, trying to get away from jaws and teeth and tail.

The mako's tail has almost equal-sized lobes. Its teeth are cone shaped and gnarled. Hemingway describes the teeth in *The Old Man and the Sea* as "shaped like a man's fingers when they are

A blue shark.

crisped like claws."

Those teeth were highly prized as earrings by the Maoris (MAH-oh-rihs), the first inhabitants of New Zealand. Two teeth could be exchanged in the marketplace for two bulls. The Maoris fished for makos from their canoes, but not with hooks that might damage those valuable teeth. They attracted the makos with dumped fish, lassooed them, and dragged them ashore — simple as roping a steer.

Makos are thought to be ovoviviparous. (They bear live young from eggs hatched inside their bodies.) They can grow to be thirteen feet long, and the Shark Attack File* charges them with eighteen attacks on humans.

Among the many other species that live in the temperate oceans is the **great white shark**. The great white: its name alone — any of its names — is enough to make men shiver.

*The Mote Marine Laboratory in Sarasota, Florida, maintains detailed records of shark attacks which occur throughout the world.

The great white is also called the white pointer, the maneater, the great white death. It is said if you come face to face with one in the ocean it is the last thing you will ever see. Jacques Cousteau did come face to face with one once when he was diving. For some reason it was as frightened as he was. It turned a somersault in the water, and swam quickly away. But this close enounter was the exception, and a lucky exception for Captain Cousteau.

The great white is strange among sharks. It does not bump or nudge before it bites. It simply bites. One unnerving habit it has is to stick its great head out of the water and look around — as if searching. Searching for what? The largest great white caught was twenty-one feet long. It was taken off the coast of Cuba in 1941 and probably weighed over five thousand pounds. The largest great white

The head and jaws of a great white shark showing three rows of teeth. When the shark loses teeth from the front row, new teeth move forward to fill the spaces from the row behind.

ever caught in western North America was eighteen feet and one half inch long and weighed forty-one hundred and fifty pounds. It was found off the coast of Catalina Island in California in June of 1976. Its body was sent to Sea World in San Diego where it was examined, frozen (to stop it from decomposing) and put on display for a year and half. Its liver weighed almost six hundred pounds and its heart weighed ten pounds. It was ten feet, two inches around the middle, and its wide-open jaws measured two feet, three inches up and down, and one foot, ten inches across. That's big enough to swallow a grown woman whole.

Frank Mundus, who operates a shark fishing boat on the east coast of the United States, caught a great white that was more than seventeen feet long. Its mounted head now stares at diners who eat in a restaurant in Montauk, New York. The sight of that head should be enough to spoil the heartiest appetite.

But great whites are rare and getting rarer. In a Florida shark fishing business one hundred thousand sharks were caught in ten years. Only twenty-seven of those were great whites.

Valerie Taylor, a world-famous shark photographer, says, "It is expensive to find a great white today. In twenty years it may be impossible." Man is destroying much of the giant shark's natural food sources — seals, sea turtles, even whales. And the great whites themselves are being sought out and killed for thrills. Their teeth and their jaws are hot-selling items just about anywhere.

The whites are really gray-brown above with white undersides. They are massive creatures, bulky and stiff bodied. Each pectoral fin has a black tip, and the tail and dorsal fin are dark on the lower edges. There is a black spot in what could be called the armpit. The great white's teeth are large, jagged, and so sharp that Florida Indians once used them for arrowheads. No wonder: they come as big as two inches in length.

Great whites have been responsible for thirty-three attacks on humans. The greatest number of these took place off the waters of Northern California.

The island prison of Alcatraz sits on a rock in San Francisco Bay. When it was in use, it was said to be escape proof — not only because of its walls and guards, or because of the deadly ocean currents. The very thought that great white sharks could be cruising in the bay

Above: A great white shark arriving at Sea World in San Diego for examination.
Below: A frozen great white shark being prepared for display at Sea World in San Diego.

must have been reason enough not to try swimming for shore. As the saying went:

"Don't jump off the rock, my friend,
The water's cold and deep.
And the sharks are waiting there, my friend,
Those sharks that never sleep."

Great whites have a bad reputation. Often it is deserved. Sometimes it isn't.

In June 1968 *Life* magazine ran a picture article. It showed a diver being attacked and killed by a great white. The diver, they said, was rushed to the hospital, but he did not survive.

Later, the people at *Life* found out they had been fooled. They had bought pictures of an attack that never happened. A movie had been made called *Shark*. For its part in the movie — the title role — a bull shark was drugged. It was dragged through the water toward a diver. Lots of nice red ketchup was dripped all around, and there were good flurries of pink water and streaming pink bubbles.

Nobody was hurt in the film except the shark. It died.

Normally the great whites go about their business and leave humans alone — if humans leave them alone. But great whites have a dangerous habit of coming sometimes to prowl close to shore.

In 1966 a thirteen-year-old boy was attacked thirty yards from the beach in five feet of water. The shark first bit his left thigh, then

went for his right leg. Six men tried to pull the boy to shore, but the shark held on. One of them clubbed it on the head with a surfboard. It still held on. The boy was dragged onto the beach, and the white came along. Its jaws had to be pried open. The boy was saved, and his legs were too. The shark was killed.

One Australian diver, Henri Bsource, lost his left leg to a great white, not once but twice. The first leg was bitten off in 1964. His second left leg, an artificial one, was bitten off again four years later while he was filming from a rubber dingy. Bource still dives, but now he leaves his new artificial leg on shore.

White sharks spell danger for other sharks too. The stomach of one large one held two dead sharks — one that was six feet long and another that was seven. Rondolet, a French naturalist who lived in 1558, seemed fascinated by great whites and what they were able to swallow. He wrote of one that he had seen with "a throat so big that a large and fat man could easily enter it, such that if one held the mouth open dogs could easily go inside to eat what they might find in the stomach."

No great whites have been successfully kept in captivity. One that was more than eight and a half feet long lived for only thirty-five hours in a tank at Marineland, Florida. Sea World in San Diego, California, kept a small four-and-a-half-foot one for five days.

Few people have ever seen a great white swimming deep in its

A great white shark.

own sunless, windless world. Those who have feel a sense of awe and wonder. In his book *Blue Meridian*, Peter Mathiessen describes one that he saw as "a silent thing of merciless serenity."

More people are now trying to join the select few who have seen that pale shadow in the world of darkness.

For money — a lot of money — arrangements can be made for a man or woman to photograph "Big Whitey" from an underwater steel cage. For the money, they get to see that massive head; that conical snout; that eye, black as a hole. They may get to feel the cage shudder as one of the greatest creatures on earth rams itself against the bars. They may be able to look into that gaping canyon of a mouth. Those who have seen it say it's worth what it cost — and in 1976 it cost four thousand dollars! Today the price may be a great deal more.

The warm sub-tropical and tropical oceans are home to countless species of sharks. Once again, their different habits help to ease the competition.

Thresher sharks are dark brown or gray above and lighter below. The unusual part of this shark is its tail. The upper lobe is especially long, often as long as the shark's entire body. The thresher may use its tail to round up fish, or to flip them into its mouth. It may even use its tail to skim sea birds off the surface and down its throat.

One fisherman is said to have had his head slashed off by a thresher's tail. The story goes that he leaned

Above: A thresher shark.
Opposite page: A hammerhead shark.

over the rail of his boat to see what he'd caught on his line. What he'd caught was a thresher. Swish! A headless fisherman! That is how the story goes as told by a friend of a friend who knew the man it happened to. And the friend swears it's true.

Threshers are also called foxsharks, foxtails, swingletails or sickletails. None are on file as having attacked anyone, not even the one that chopped off the head of the friend of my friend's friend!

Some sharks look alike. It is easy to confuse one kind with another. The thresher's tail makes it different. The shape of the head does the same thing for the hammerhead.

Hammerhead sharks are like something out of a nightmare, or a science-fiction movie. Their long, flattened, hammer-shaped heads have an eye set at each end. Sometimes the heads are so wide that the space between the left eye and the right eye may be as much as three feet.

There are nine species of hammerheads. The smallest, about five feet long, are called bonnetheads. They are harmless and live in the shallow tropical waters of bays and inlets. But the large hammerheads are not harmless. The Shark Attack File says they have attacked both boats and swimmers. One huge creature was found to contain human remains and articles of clothing.

No one is sure why hammerheads have heads shaped in this strange way. Perhaps it is to give lift and agility. Or it may be that the electricity-sensing ampullae of Lorenzini have better sensitivity

when they are spread like this, over a wide area. When this shark swims along the bottom, its head swings from side to side like a minesweeper. Stingrays, which bury themselves in sand, are the hammerhead's favorite food. Ninety-six poisonous barbs were found in one hammerhead's jaw, mouth, and head. Maybe they'd slowed the hammerhead a little, but they surely hadn't stopped it.

Nurse sharks also live in tropical seas. They are slow, rather drab, and generally harmless. "Nasal barbels," like soft tusks, come down from their snouts. Nurses are brownish in color and can grow as big as fourteen feet. Since they are able to breathe without moving, they often lie half-hidden on the bottom. They don't look at all ferocious lying there, and divers are sometimes tempted to prod them — just to see what happens. A thirteen-year-old boy saw what happened. He had his arm bitten when he pulled on the tail of a little two-footer.

Tiger sharks also like warm, tropical oceans. They often swim together in groups, the markings on their backs like bars of sunshine and shadow. Their snouts are squarish, their teeth curve to the side and their tempers are ferocious.

The largest tiger shark ever caught was eighteen feet. The Shark Attack File shows that they have made twenty-seven attacks on humans.

Two men were killed in 1937. Their legs, parts of their arms, and the hand of one were found the next day in an eight-hundred-and-

Right: A nurse shark.
Opposite page: A tiger shark.

fifty-pound tiger shark. In 1967 a spear diver in Australia was "bitten in half" in a tiger shark's jaws.

Tiger sharks are basically shy and don't care for the company of other sharks. It is often difficult to get them to eat in captivity, which is strange because in the wild a tiger shark will eat almost anything. The head of a cow was found in one, the head of a horse in another, the head of a crocodile in still another. Even elephants are not safe. In 1959 a crazed elephant plunged into the ocean off South Africa. It was torn apart before it could escape.

Fishermen who trap their fish in nets say it is the tiger sharks who feed most often on other captured sharks.

Stewart Springer, one of the world's leading shark researchers, holds a strange record. And it must surely be the record for the most sharks ever caught on one hook. He caught a tiger shark at the mouth of the Mississippi River. In its stomach was a bull shark. In the bull's stomach was a blacktip shark. In the blacktip's stomach was a dogfish. There they were, the four of them — one inside the other, like Chinese boxes.

Tiger sharks are ovoviviparous. Their litters are large. One gave birth to eighty-two pups.

The tiger stripes that make this shark easy to recognize are more noticeable in the young sharks. As they get older, the markings fade so the shark looks almost gray or gray-brown.

Above: The head of a whale shark.
Below: A skin diver riding a whale shark.

The stripes and spots on the back of the giant **whale shark** stay bright for all of its days. The whale shark likes tropical oceans too. This is another shark that is easy to identify. First there is its size. It is immense. It can grow up to forty-two feet. That makes it about as big as a bus! The yellow stripes and dots aren't hard to spot either. Even the giant tail is spotted.

Whale sharks eat plankton and small fish. Their mouths are on the front of their heads instead of being underslung. Spongy tissue lies between their gill arches inside their mouths. This acts as a trap in which to catch the plankton. Whale sharks will also eat squid and even tuna. They have been seen "upright" in the water with their heads sticking out. They bob up and down with their mouths open, swallowing whatever swims in.

Big and slow-moving, they often get in the way of boats — a sad thing for both the boats and the sharks.

Whale sharks are rare. Little is known about them. A few years ago a whale shark egg was found in the net of a trawler. The fisherman heard sounds inside, slit the egg open, and found a whale shark embryo. Add one fact to what we do know about this, the largest of all fish: it is oviparous.

Whale sharks appear to be harmless to humans. Skin divers have climbed on their backs. Jacques Cousteau even made a film of his divers getting a ride on one, holding on to the gigantic dorsal fin.

Bull sharks are remarkable sharks. They live in tropical oceans, but they also live in bays and rivers. They can swim from full-strength salt water to full-strength fresh and come to no harm. Some species of bony fish, such as salmon and eels, can do this too. But the bull shark is the only species of shark that can.

Bulls grow to a length of ten feet. They have wide heads, short rounded snouts, and they are dangerous wherever they are — in sea, lake, or river.

In the 1930's bull sharks swam a thousand miles up the Mississippi River. A fisherman in Illinois was puzzled because his nets kept getting ripped and torn. When he saw a bull shark he was puzzled

no longer. Today, the locks and dams on the Mississippi make its upper reaches safe from sharks. Bulls are still found one hundred and sixty miles up the Atchafalaya River in Louisiana. They swim too in the Ganges, the holy river of India. When pilgrims bathe in its sacred waters they are easy prey for sharks. The Ganges is also presented with the bodies of the dead. And the bulls aren't fussy. They take the dead bodies too.

Bull sharks peril swimmers in inland lakes. In Lake Nicaragua several people have been attacked. The bulls have killed hippos in African rivers, and buffalos, and anything else they can find. They are commonly found close to land and have been caught off bridges and piers. Bulls are the sharks most responsible for the fatal attacks off South African beaches. Those beaches that have been netted against sharks are now safe. In the period between 1966 and 1972 more than seven thousand sharks were trapped and died in the protective nets off South African beaches. But the strange thing is that as many seemed to be caught going back out as were caught coming in. What a scary thought. Somehow they swam around the nets, took a look around, and decided to head back for the open seas. And the swimmers swam and splashed and felt perfectly secure. And for some reason they were. There have been only three shark attacks since the netting was put up, and they all happened outside the netted area.

Bull sharks will pass up hooks baited with tuna or bonita in favor of a hook baited with another shark. Sometimes one will swallow another hooked bull shark whole: Then it can't free itself, and it is caught too.

Still left untold is the story of the saw shark, the leopard, the bramble, and the swell; and that of the frill shark, the porbeagle, the wobbegong, and the angel; and the others. There is not enough space to write about all of them.

They live in the waters of the world and they are all extraordinary. They are what they are, and so they do what they do — for reasons that we, who are not sharks, do not always like or understand.

A bull shark.

ONCE THERE WERE DINOSAURS
CHAPTER SEVEN

Sharks are the creatures that humans love to hate. It seems there is nothing too terrible to do to one, dead or alive. People who wouldn't kick a dog will stab a dying shark. They will poke out its eyes, or chop off its tail. There is a strange madness that overcomes people when they deal with sharks. They have fed them hand grenades, hidden in bait; and they have cheered when the sharks were blown to bits. Nice, kindly fishermen have been known to put cans of drain cleaner into shark bait. They thought it was justice when the sharks died in agony, their insides burned away. There is no Society for the Prevention of Cruelty to Sharks, and no one feels the need to start one. Sharks eat people. To some, that seems reason

Above: A dead shark being eaten by starfish.

Left: A captured tiger shark.

Following page: A blue shark swimming among a school of small fish.

enough to kill them — to kill them in the ugliest ways possible.

It is true that sharks have eaten people, or at least taken bites out of them. People have died as the result of shark attacks. Sharks attack out of fear, or to protect their territory, or because they are predators. It is their nature to search for food. We look like their kind of food. We may look like what we're not — seals or sea lions. But sharks don't kill humans for fun, or because they hate us, or for revenge. Somehow, the sharks' motives seem cleaner than ours are when we kill them.

Some people don't want to understand why there should be sharks at all. What good are they, they ask? Some taste all right. But it's a hassle catching them. They'll try to bite the fisherman and maybe succeed. People say there are other fish that taste better. And who knows, this shark that they're thinking of eating may have eaten a person. Would this make them cannibals?

There are people who think it would be fine if sharks were simply wiped out.

Of course it would not be fine.

In the wonderful cycle of the underwater world, everything floats in its own balance. The drifting plankton is food for small fish. Small fish are food for larger ones. The large fish feed the giant predators like the sharks and the killer whales. Nothing is wasted.

When a shark dies, its body drops to the bottom. What is not eaten by fellow sharks and fish is picked clean by the crabs. Other

scavengers finish it off. Anything left crumbles on the ocean floor. It becomes nutrients which feed the plankton. The plankton feeds the small fish, which feed the larger fish, which feed the predators. Life in the sea, as on land, is a complete and perfect cycle. No part of the cycle, big or small, is unimportant. The humble plankton indirectly or directly feeds the great giants of the sea. In death, they return the life and energy they were given.

Sharks prefer to prey on food that is easily caught. They will chase the slower fish that lag behind the others. These are often the weak or sickly ones. The sharks do in the seas what the great cats and other predators do on land. They remove the feeble, the frail, the unfit. So they protect future fish generations by not allowing bad genes to be passed on. They weed out the weak and make more space and a greater food supply for the strong and the healthy.

When people want land they take it. They have pushed the creatures from the forest. Traffic roars where once condors soared. Now human eyes are turning to the seas to meet human needs. But the ocean predators are there. They will not be as easily removed as the predators of land and air.

In 1854 Chief Seattle asked,

"What is man without the beasts? If all the beasts were gone, men would die from a great loneliness of spirit. For whatever happens to the beasts soon happens to man. All things are connected."

Once there were dinosaurs.
The dinosaurs are gone.
There are still sharks.
Bluer than blue, darker than dark, soundless and sleepless they
swim on .... to a time that is beyond our knowing, from a time past

INDEX

BIBLIOGRAPHY

Brown, Theo W. *Sharks, The Silent Savages*. Boston: Little Brown and Co., 1973.

Budker, Paul. *The Life of Sharks*. New York: Columbia University Press, 1971.

Burgess, Robert F. *The Sharks*. New York: Doubleday and Co., 1970.

Butler, Jean Campbell. *Danger — Shark*. Boston: Little Brown and Co., 1964.

Clark, Eugenie. *The Lady and the Sharks*. New York: Harper & Row, 1969.

Copps, Dale. *Savage Survivor*. Milwaukee: Westwind Press, 1976.

Cousteau, Jacques-Yves, and Philippe. *The Shark: Spendid Savage of the Sea*. New York: Doubleday and Co., 1970.

Dennis, Felix, ed. *Man-Eating Sharks*. Secaucus: Castle Books, 1976.

Ellis, Richard. *The Book of Sharks*. New York: Grosset & Dunlap, 1976.

Lineweaver, Thomas H. III, and Backus, Richard H. *The Natural History of Sharks*. Philadelphia: J. B. Lippencott Company, 1970.

Zim, Herbert S. *Sharks*. New York: William Morrow and Co., 1966.

Acknowledgements

The author gratefully acknowledges the help of:

The entire aquarium department at Sea World in San Diego.

Dr. Lawrence G. Barnes,
Curator of Vertebrate Paleontology,
Museum of Natural History,
Los Angeles, California.